Relationships

Robyn Hardyman

PowerKiDS press™

New York

Published in 2010 by The Rosen Publishing Group Inc.
29 East 21st Street, New York, NY 10010

First Edition

Design: Nick Leggett and Paul Myerscough
Editor: Sarah Eason
Picture research: Maria Joannou
Consultant: Sue Beck MSc, BSc
Commissioning Editor for Wayland: Jennifer Sanderson

Library of Congress Cataloging-in-Publication Data

Hardyman, Robyn.
Relationships / Robyn Hardyman.
p. cm. -- (Being healthy, feeling great)
Includes index.
ISBN 978-1-61532-371-5 (library binding)
ISBN 978-1-61532-380-7 (paperback)
ISBN 978-1-61532-381-4 (6-pack)
1. Social skills in children--Juvenile literature. 2. Interpersonal relations--Juvenile literature.
3. Children--Family relationships--Juvenile literature. 4. Friendship--Juvenile literature. I. Title.
HQ783.H37 2010
177'.62--dc22
2009023892

Photographs:
The publisher would like to thank the following for permission to reproduce photographs:
Alamy Images: Moodboard 20, John Powell Photographer 8; Corbis: Ephraim Ben-Shimon 6,
Heide Benser/Zefa 16, LWA-Dann Tardif 23; Fotolia: Galina Barskaya 12, 31; Getty Images:
Iconica/ColorBlind Images 25, The Image Bank/Larry Dale Gordon 13; Istockphoto: Asiseeit 21,
Digitalskillet 1, 7, 9, 28, Andrea Laurita 11; Rex Features: Francis Dean 18; Shutterstock: Yuri
Arcurs 4, Rick Becker-Leckrone 14, Mikael Damkier 22, Elena Elisseeva 17, Miodrag Gajic 26,
Monkey Business Images 5, 27, Amy Myers 24, Anita Patterson Peppers 10, Larry St. Pierre 15,
Lisa F. Young 19. Cover: Shutterstock/Digitalskillet.

Manufactured in China

CPSIA Compliance Information: Batch #WAW0102PK: For Further Information

contact Rosen Publishing, New York, New York at 1-800-237-9932

Contents

People need people

Everyone needs other people! You have relationships with many people, at home, school, and in your community. Your relationships with others are an important part of making your life healthy and happy.

You can learn a lot from the different people you meet. Getting along with other people is satisfying and fun. Your closest relationships can also be a source of support and help whenever you feel that you need it.

Ups and downs

Relationships can sometimes be difficult. At home, you may feel that your parents do not treat you fairly—or perhaps you often argue with your siblings. If your parents separate, your family relationships will begin to change. You may have to make new relationships in a stepfamily.

At school, it can sometimes be hard to make and keep friends. Friends often break up and make up.

A good friend will be there for good times and bad times.

As you go through life, you need to work at all kinds of different relationships. You have to get along with different teachers. You may be part of a sports team, so you need to learn to work well with your team members. You may have virtual relationships with people on the Internet.

Getting it wrong

Sometimes, relationships go badly wrong. Bullying, as well as negative peer pressure, when people try to get someone to do things they do not want to do, are problems that people often come across as they are growing up. Everyone needs skills to deal with these kinds of problems.

Getting it right

This book will help you to make the most of all your relationships. It will help you to identify any problems and will show you what you can do to make things better.

We live life to the full when we have relationships with people of all ages.

5

Parents and guardians

There are many kinds of family. In a traditional family, two parents live together with their children. However, many children live in single-parent families, stepfamilies, foster families, extended families, or adoptive families. Your family may look different from other families, but it is still a special and important place for you to feel loved and secure as you grow up.

There for you

Your closest relationships are often those you have with your parents or other main guardians. These are the people who love and look after you. They help you to learn, and support you as you grow up.

Sometimes you will not see eye to eye with your parents or guardians.

Even though your guardians and parents love you, and you love them, you may not always get along so well. For example, they may get cross with you if you do something wrong. Or you may get annoyed with them if you think they are being unfair. These types of problems are normal and they can be worked out. They do not last for long.

Talk about it

Abuse is when someone hurts you, either physically or emotionally. If a parent or guardian abuses you in any way, it is important to get help. Talk to another trusted adult, such as a teacher at school.

There for them

"Give and take" is an important part of all relationships. Most parents and guardians give a lot of love and time to their children. You can find lots of ways to give something back. Being helpful is a good start. You could help out with household chores and be ready to go to school on time. Small things make a big difference.

Saying thank you to your parents and guardians makes them feel appreciated. Telling them about things that matter to you will bring you closer. If you do have problems, talking calmly to them about how you feel will help to solve them.

Being open with one another helps to bring people closer.

Brothers and sisters

Brothers and sisters can be a lot of fun! You can do things together and enjoy being with someone who knows you really well. A relationship with a sibling can teach you a lot. It will prepare you for other types of relationships, at school and with friends.

Sibling rivalry

Everyone is different. Brothers and sisters may have very different personalities. Because of this, each sibling may have a slightly different relationship with their parents or guardians.

You may feel jealous of your brother or sister sometimes. This can make you feel sad or angry. It can cause arguments, or even fights, with your sibling. These feelings are perfectly normal. When you argue a lot with your brother or sister, it is known as sibling rivalry.

Everyone argues with their siblings at times. Talking calmly about how you feel will help you to sort things out.

A sibling can be a good friend who is always there for you.

Jealousy is not the only reason for sibling rivalry. Maybe your big brother has no time to play with you any more. Or perhaps your little sister keeps borrowing your belongings without asking. These things can be upsetting or annoying.

Dealing with sibling rivalry

Sibling rivalry can make you feel really miserable. If problems are not resolved, it can last for a long time—even for years. Always try to talk to your brother or sister if they upset or annoy you. Listen to what they have to say, too. Try to work things out so you are both happy and can get along again.

Healthy Hints

Words hurt

Words can be very hurtful. People often remember the things you say to them long after you have forgotten them. Try to think before you speak. If you think it will hurt your brother or sister, do not say it!

You may need to talk to your parents or guardians about how you feel. If you feel left out, try asking them to spend some special time with you. If you cannot work things out with your sibling, ask your parents to help.

Family breakup

It is hard when families break up, especially for children. Family breakups bring lots of changes, which children need to get used to. Sometimes family relationships may change. Children may have to divide their time between two homes. In time, they may even have to live with a stepfamily.

Big changes

If your parents separate, you will probably feel very sad for a while. You may worry that the separation is because of something you did. Do not worry, this is unlikely to be the case. Breaking up is usually because of problems between parents.

A family breakup is always sad, but it is never your fault.

You may worry about what will happen next. You will probably miss the parent who is no longer living with you. You may need to move to a new house or school. These are big changes but you do not have to make them alone. Your parents and the rest of your family will help you. Eventually, everything will settle down and life will begin to feel normal again.

Keep talking

Try to keep talking to your parents about your feelings. Do not let your worries build up inside. Talk to other trusted adults and friends, too. They will be able to reassure you that everything will get better.

Stepfamilies

One day, your parents may meet someone new. They may decide to live with or marry that person. When this happens, you will need to get used to living with a stepparent and maybe stepsiblings, too. You may find this hard at first, but try to remember, your own parents are still there for you.

New family relationships can be rewarding.

Changing times

Every family has its own way of doing things. In a stepfamily, routines—such as mealtimes and bedtimes—may change. If there is anything you disagree with, talk about it with your parent and your stepparent. That way, you should all be able to agree on what to do.

The extended family

Many children have relationships with people in their extended family. They may also have family gatherings with grandparents, uncles, aunts, and cousins. The times they spend together are really important, and they can also be a lot of fun, too.

Grandparents

There is probably quite a big age gap between you and your grandparents. Even so, you can have a great relationship. Relationships do not depend on age. Everyone has got something to give, whether they are old or young.

If you see a lot of your grandparents, you will get to know each other well. They can be good friends who give you lots of useful advice. Grandparents often have more time to spare than busy parents or guardians.

Healthy Hints

Helping out

You have lots to give to your grandparents, too. You can help to keep them company. They will be happy when you tell them about the different things you do at school and home. You can also help them with little jobs they may find difficult to do.

Relationships between grandparents and their grandchildren can be very special.

In an extended family, there is always someone to share good times with.

They have time to do fun activities with you. They can teach you new skills, such as cooking or gardening. If you have a problem, a grandparent is often a good person to talk to. They have had a lot of experience and they may be very wise. They can help you to work things out.

Aunts, uncles, and cousins

Spending time with your aunts, uncles, and cousins can make you feel part of something bigger. You know that there are many other people who love you and who will support you.

Some family gatherings can be like a big party! Your aunts and uncles may have fun stories to tell you about your parents when they were young, too. You may also find that you have a lot in common with your cousins. They may be a similar age to you and you can become good friends for life.

Friends

Relationships with friends can be very special. It is important to have friends to share fun times with. Having a good friend, who you can talk to about anything, is a great support, too.

Different friendships

You cannot be best friends with everyone. You may have friends at school, who you never see outside of school.

You may have friendships with people who do the same activities as you, such as swimming or drama, but you may never invite them home. These friendships may be very casual, but they are still important. It is good to have different friends as you grow up, as well as a few close ones. That way, you learn to have a lot of relationships with all kinds of different people.

Sharing times with a group of friends makes growing up easier—and a lot more fun.

Good friends

A relationship with a good friend can last a lifetime. Good friends like and accept each other just as they are. They often spend lots of time together. They may like the same things, for instance, sports or dancing, or the same kinds of music or clothes.

Good friends respect each other, and they know that they can trust each other, too. They can share their thoughts, feelings, and problems, knowing that they will be listened to. Even if they disagree, they can work things out by talking about them.

Making friends

Sometimes, it can be difficult to make friends, especially if you are very shy. Fortunately, there are ways to make it easier. Try joining a club or sports team. You will meet people there who have the same interests as you, which makes it easier to get to know them.

Joining a sports team is a good way to make new friends.

Healthy Hints

Feeling shy

Sometimes, people look confident but they may feel shy, just like you.

Breaking up and making up

It is normal for friendships to go through difficult times. Sometimes, friends break up. They argue or stop speaking to each other and they stop spending time together.

Breaking up with friends feels horrible, even if it does not last long. It can make you—and your friend—feel unhappy and worried. It is not good to keep breaking up with a friend. In time, too much conflict can spoil a friendship.

Most friendships break up occasionally.

Healthy Hints

Breaking up for good

It is not always possible to make up with a friend. You may need to move on and make a new friend instead.

Breaking up

Friends break up for many different reasons. Usually, one or both of them feels very hurt or angry about something. For instance, if a friend teases you, you might feel annoyed and shout at him or her. If a friend starts spending time with someone else, you may feel left out and stop talking to him or her.

16

Making up is much better than breaking up with friends!

Stop and think

The reasons for ending friendships always seem important at the time. Later, you may wish that you had not argued. Sometimes, you just need time to stop and think about things.

Did your friend really mean to upset you? Did you say or do something unhelpful, too? Can you think of a way in which you can both make it better? If you do this early, you may be able to work things out with a friend. You can avoid rushing into saying or doing something that you regret later.

Making up

If you have a problem with a friend, always try to talk to them about it. Tell your friend how you feel and ask how he or she feels, too. Perhaps your friend was unkind because he or she has problems at home. This may not be an excuse, but it could be a good reason why you argued. You may decide to forget all about it and make up.

If you have hurt your friend, say that you are sorry. Let him or her know that you still want to be friends.

We are all different

Everyone is different. We look different and we have different personalities. Some people are more outgoing than others. Others are more shy. People also have different interests, opinions, and beliefs. Our many differences are important. They make the world a really interesting place.

Equality for all

Everyone is equal. Another person's customs may seem strange to you, but they are simply different. No one is any better or any worse than anyone else, just because they wear clothes that you may not like, eat foods you have not heard of, or have different beliefs. Everyone deserves your respect, just as you deserve respect, too.

Clothes are just on the outside. It is what is inside that counts!

A different point of view

A person who has different customs from yours may find some of your customs just as strange as you find theirs! Try to think about that if you find them different or odd.

People with disabilities

Many people in the world suffer from a disability. Disabilities can be physical, such as being blind or deaf, or being paralyzed. If someone's legs are paralyzed, they may use a wheelchair.

Some people may have learning disabilities. They may not be able to attend school, or if they do, they may need extra support. Others are born with conditions such as Down's Syndrome. They often have learning disabilities and other health problems.

Lots of people with a disability are mocked by other people. This is hurtful, unfair, and very wrong. People with disabilities want to be treated like other people. Just like anyone else, they deserve to live a full, happy life and to enjoy lots of good, respectful relationships with other people.

Learn and share

Relationships teach us a lot. If we make friends with someone who is

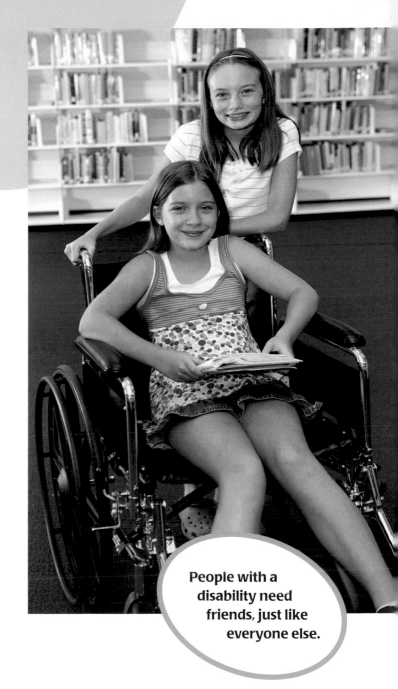

People with a disability need friends, just like everyone else.

very different from us, we can learn all kinds of interesting ideas. We may enjoy new, fun experiences. We can share our thoughts and ideas with our friend, too. It can be a great friendship that lasts forever.

Peer pressure

Your peers are people who are the same age as you. They may be people you know from school or the community, or they may be your friends. When your peers try to get you to do something they want you to do, this is known as peer pressure.

Some peer pressure is positive. A friend may encourage you to work harder at school or practice more in your chosen sport. But sometimes, peer pressure can be negative. This is when someone tries to persuade you to do something you feel uncomfortable with. Perhaps they want you to skip school or to become involved in bullying someone else.

Healthy competition and peer pressure can help you to achieve more.

Why do people give in?

Everyone wants to be liked. Sometimes, people give in to negative peer pressure because they want others to like them. Pleasing their peers and being popular seems more important than doing the right thing.

Resist the pressure

You can resist negative peer pressure. Standing up to it can make you feel good, because you are sticking up for what you believe in. This is more important than being liked by someone who has different values from yours. Remember, a good friend will never try to make you do something you do not want to do.

If you feel under pressure, think for a minute before you do or say anything. Think, "Do I really want to do this? Is it unsafe or unkind, or against the rules?" This helps you to figure out what is most important to you. It can be difficult to do, but it is worth it.

Be clear

If you decide that you do not want to do something, say "No" clearly. Be confident when you speak. Remember, you have made a decision you can be proud of.

It can feel hard to resist peer pressure, but you will feel proud to make the right choice.

Healthy Hints

Stand up for yourself

You may think that someone will dislike you if you stand up to negative peer pressure. But most people respect those who stand up for themselves.

21

Bullying

Bullying is when someone hurts another person on purpose. It may happen once or it may occur lots of times. Bullying is very hurtful. It is important to stop it as soon as possible.

Different forms of bullying

Bullying can be physical or nonphysical. Physical bullying is when someone hurts your body, for instance, by pushing, hitting, or kicking you. If a bully steals any of your belongings, this is physical bullying, too.

Nonphysical bullying is often verbal. The bully may call you names, make fun of you, or tell lies about you to other people. Bullying can happen from a distance. Cyberbullying is when a bully leaves you a nasty message on your cell phone or e-mail, or if they write lies about you on a social networking website.

Whatever form it takes, bullying makes its victims feel sad and frightened. The effects can last for a very long time.

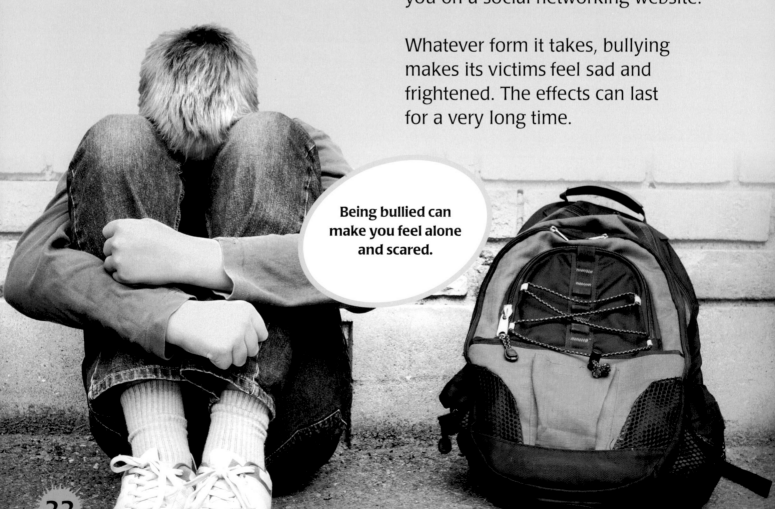

Being bullied can make you feel alone and scared.

A trusted adult can help to bring bullying to a stop.

Dealing with bullies

If you are being bullied, it is important to know that it is not your fault. No one deserves to be bullied and no one asks for it. Remember, you are not alone. There are lots of people, such as your parents or your teacher, who can help to stop the bullying. Tell them about it as soon as it starts.

It is usually better to walk away from a bully. Go somewhere safe, where there are other people around. Bullies lose their confidence when there are other people nearby and they will probably leave you alone.

Do not be tempted to fight back—this can make things worse. Try to stay out of the bully's way, and avoid him or her as much as you can.

A different point of view

Bullies must be stopped, but they need help, too. Many bullies have problems of their own, and they feel bad about themselves. They try to make themselves feel better by hurting other people through bullying.

Team relationships

Being in a team is a good way to meet other people and to have fun. You might be in a sports team, or in a drama group in your local community. Perhaps you are in a group at school, working on an art or science project. Whatever group you are in, you will have relationships with several different people. Learning to work together is very satisfying. When you do well as a team, you all feel fantastic.

Team spirit

A team is most successful when every member feels valued. You can help by saying, "Congratulations!" when someone in your team does well.

Negative criticism does not help a team. It makes people feel worried. Remember, everyone is different, with different strengths and weaknesses. In a football team, one person may be a great lineman, but a weak quarterback. In a project group at school, someone might find it hard to add, but be really good at writing down results. Everyone in a team has something positive to give. If they find something hard, they may just need a little help, so they can get better.

When you work hard as a team, you can have a lot of fun.

A good team member respects the good things that another person can do—and helps out if someone finds something hard.

Team leaders

Most teams have a leader. This person is often chosen from your peer group because they have great skills to lead the team. A good team leader is able to tell other people what needs to be done, and makes sure that everyone has what they need. Good team leaders also help every team member to feel that they are doing a good job. Listening to your team leader and showing respect are important parts of being in a team.

Healthy Hints

Listening

If you are in a sports team, your coach may be your team leader. Always listen to what he or she tells you and always try your best. If you have a good relationship with your coach, you will learn more and perform much better.

Virtual relationships

Young people often use the Internet to chat with their friends or to make new friends. People can use e-mail, chat rooms, and social networking sites to share information about themselves and their interests with other people.

On the Internet, you are able to have relationships with lots of different people. You may know some of the people from school or your community. You may not know new online friends very well. They may seem like friends, but really they are almost strangers.

Virtual relationships can seem very real, but they are not the same as the relationships you have with people in your day-to-day life. It can be hard to know exactly who a new "friend" is, or to trust all they say. Be careful and make sure that you stay safe.

Virtual friendships can be fun—but real friends are even better!

How to stay safe online

The first rule to stay safe online is to make sure that your parents or guardians know that you are using the Internet. It can be helpful to agree on the different sites you can visit when you are online. Agree a time limit, too. And always stick to the rules! Let your parents know your password, but never give it to anyone else, not even to a close friend.

Never give out any personal information on the Internet, such as your address, telephone number, or your photograph. Social networking sites often ask for lots of personal information. If you are allowed to use a social networking site, make sure only your friends can see your profile.

Always let your parents or guardians know when you are online.

Healthy Hints

Keep safe

Never, ever go alone to meet someone you have met on the Internet. If you really want to meet them, always take a trusted adult with you and go to a safe place where there are other people.

Relationship network

You have relationships with lots of different people; in your family, at school, and in the community. Here are two fun activities to see exactly who is who in your relationship network.

Part 1: Family

Look at the diagram of the family tree below, and then use it to make your own family tree. You may not have all these relatives or you may have more. That is fine; just leave parts out or add new names when you need to. Instead of writing "me," write your own name. Then write all the names of your other relatives, too. You will be surprised how large the "tree" grows!

Part 2: Friends

Create a network of your friends. Draw a circle in the middle of the page. Write your name inside it.

Now organize your friends into groups, for example, "classmates," "judo club," and "scout camp." Draw a circle for each group. Write the group name in the circle, at the top.

Write the name of all the friends that belong in each group. Some people may go in more than one circle! Draw lines between the group circles and the circle with your name. See how many different friends you have.

Quiz

How good are your relationship skills? Try this quick quiz to find out.

1 It is recess on your first day at a new school. Do you:

a) Stand around feeling shy, hoping that someone will talk to you?

b) Look friendly and wander around the playground to see who looks friendly?

c) Go up to a group of people you think look interesting and introduce yourself with a smile?

2 Your mom will not let you stay up late on weeknights. Do you:

a) Shout at her that it is not fair, and lock yourself in your bedroom?

b) Ask her why she will not let you, and tell her calmly that your friends are allowed to?

c) Suggest that she lets you stay up later for two weeks as a trial and agree to take a rest if you feel tired?

3 Your best friend has gone off with a new person in class. Do you:

a) Decide never to speak to your friend again?

b) Tell your friend that you are upset, and then look for a new friend?

c) Ask your friend and the new person over for a sleepover, so you can all be friends together?

4 Your football team has lost an important game. Do you:

a) Shout at the quarterback who fumbled the ball?

b) Say nothing and hope that no one blames you too much?

c) Cheer everyone up by pointing out the good parts of their game and remind them that there is always another chance to win?

Answers

Mostly **as**: You could do with practicing your relationship skills a little more. Keep reading this book, it will give you lots of ideas.

Mostly **bs**: You have some good ideas, and you are trying to be friendly. If you work on your relationship skills more, your relationships can be even better.

Mostly **cs**: Congratulations! You have great relationship skills. If you want to find out more, read different books and visit websites that can give you even more information about relationships.

Glossary

adoptive families Families that have adopted a child. Adopted children are brought up legally by parents who did not give birth to the children.

chat rooms Places on the Internet where you can use e-mail to discuss something with other people.

community A place where people live, such as a city or town.

customs Ways of doing things that have been used for a long time.

cyberbullying Bullying using cell phones, e-mail, and the Internet.

disability Sickness, injury, or conditions that make it difficult for someone to do all the things that other people can.

Down's Syndrome A condition that some people are born with, which causes them to have learning disabilities and health problems.

extended family The family that includes grandparents, aunts, uncles, and cousins, as well as parents and siblings.

foster families Families that take care of a child, either for a short or long time, without being the child's legal parent.

learning disabilities Conditions that affect someone's ability to learn.

paralyzed When someone is unable to move part of their body.

peer pressure Pressure to behave in the same way as people your age.

personalities The type of person someone is, which is shown in the things they do and say.

separate To split up.

sibling A brother or sister.

sibling rivalry When siblings compete for the same thing, such as attention, causing them to argue.

single-parent families Families in which one parent looks after a child.

social networking site A place on the Internet where people chat to each other and exchange information.

stepfamily A family that includes one natural parent living with another adult and possibly with the other adult's children.

values Important beliefs to someone.

verbal To do with words.

victims People who are hurt by something that someone does to them.

virtual relationships Relationships with people you "meet" on the Internet.

Find out more and Web Sites

Books

How To Deal With Life In A Stepfamily by Lisa Cohn (Freespirit Publishing, 2008)

Making Smart Choices About Relationships by Matthew Robinson (Rosen Central, 2008)

Why Do Families Break Up? by Jane Bingham (Raintree, 2004)

Web Sites

Due to the changing nature of Internet links, PowerKids Press has developed an online list of Web sites related to the subject of this book. This site is updated regularly. Please use this link to access this list: http://www.powerkidslinks.com/bhfg/relate/

Index